TATTERDEMALION

TAT TER DEM ALI ON

Jennifer Londry

CHAUDIERE BOOKS | MMXV

for the good witches
Ann and Cat

The end of the affair is always death.
She's my workshop. Slippery eye,
out of the tribe of myself my breath
finds you gone. I horrify
those who stand by. I am fed.
At night, alone, I marry the bed.

Anne Sexton—*Love Poems*

Contents

BLUE PLENTY MORE

Blue

In Blue, they perch on maplewood porch swing
wait for railcar to push through. Destination:
Plenty—page 18 in a book read once. It is where
north is separated from its counterpart like a
village under quarantine, southbound line,
plague-struck clock, steel fever of birth sudden
sadness, unstoppable black kite. In the year of
the religious-tobacconists' lost calendar, in the
month of the copper leaf, the train arrived
3 seconds early, teapot bumped to the floor
lantern twisted from its hook, a mute fell
from a rooftop, split in half—Wormhole eye,
twin simpletons cut from the same startled
cloth. A dozen on board stared and counted
3 naked flowerpots knocking against a red
clapboard cottage empty. In Blue, they avoid
even numbers—suspicion's ethical wild card.
The tree shook an hour before and after the
rattle summoned tracks' hum   still. Hatboxes
burned and Frightened came back with its
head on a younger man's lap.

Plenty

A city once lived under the town. The ruin of leisure. Skipped, slid and fell into youthful cup. Rabbit-hole

with its dark chocolate eyelash, lamplight flicker, Johnny came late and mothers ran

for their little pill-box helpers, a new sexology. Utopian ease, a dunce for hire at every turn

delivered amusement for quick-witted Lords who liked to play marble games.

More

Out for a loop

around

the bend never tasted so pretty despite the hunger of the vodka

maker's lukewarm handshake.

1 / Train

Steel darts
weightless passengers on a flatbed.

Shout

Smoky window, my face, a smudge, a timestamp—
leather, noisy teacart, passports crestfallen, afterlife-kindling.
The journey warps around birch, maple, mountain ash, cabin, cabin, cabin
weird boredom.

Hush

This—
green
yellow
orange
backdrop
the shadow of its season's thin-ghost, familiar.
This is where my dead come from.

2 / The wage of Patience's war

Patience was born a third generation lunatic.

Mother.
Father.
Dead.

Not really.
Life is not that kind.

3/ Second guessing the timetable

It is with a specific aside that I must tell you …

man killed man
not the train.

All the speculations: bad weather, bad timing, deafness and pre-occupations—
bullshit—
it is not natural.

If we are lucky, we do depart with a fast urge.

It's all about aesthetics, and suicidal forms.

Now is it…
here doesn't count.

This is your story.   It began yesterday.
Are you surprised   it started without you?

Hindsight is a temporary virgin   a has-been.

4/ Baby

blacksleepblacksheepblacksleep

Patience came out blue
a sexless lump.

Not in a blanket
not in a basket
not in a clutch-feast of passion.

Nurture the child.

5/ Dueling musicians

Mama is all legs in the kitchen.
Pa is covered in mechanics.

I am the wrench between our house and the neighbour's
icebox.

Beside a blossoming magnolia, a rusty pitchfork roosts in the shadiest part
of the day.

A bucket of square nails sits next to lethargic
half ton parked in the mud.

I know the VIN because when the sky turns gunmetal it glows.

Pa reads the Sunday papers.
He's a soft spoken offender.

I swear an allegiance to a set of fast picking hands that don't look like mine.

He plucks banjo.
I play guitar. I ain't no killer, but I could be.

Motive, that's all it takes
a sly fist and a cruel inkling.

Mercy Street

Clatter hall

Grotty, hoodwinked wide and psychotic, the she-six
could not be washed pretty in the water barrel warmed by the sun that bathed them clean.
A stack of terry by the back step.

The husband heaved them into the wet dirt of his earth
cuddled each naked raw.

Youthful Seven

tucked a wisp of sweet behind the ear and stepped into the vestibule of the summerhouse
where wisteria grew wild over a Dutch door.

Inside: an ivory piano, Parsons table, cane chairs, bouquets of spring
a shared bed.

Seven belted out the words that shied them—

sissy *pussy*
ear-worm *sex-worm*

They scattered down a thin hallway where the floor pattern changed direction as it crept toward the servery in a puzzled light.

Under the steady tresses of their farmhouse kitchen, the she-six

suckled
the morning ugly
and hollered the house down.

Bully bully

Lost opportunity
to push bare skinned into snow.
Watch the surrender of her February and the cold days that burn and sink
into hollow amber eyes.

By the side of the road—
a frozen kilt, found. Red alert
fierce flashing sky earth bound.

No signs of forced entry
or broken glass—
two blocks west of the schoolyard in a basement apartment
an emotional cripple sits by a window, faces spring.

Night witch

In the cellarage beneath the lonely walkway
she danced his blushed virgin
to cinder.

Slow to burn
the condom in his pocket.
Sweet flame
a song between his tender legs.

An obsession she cannot abort, a fondness for blond plumes
and cold cockcrow
paralysis.

New neighbours

He said she would love it when she saw it.
The house he bought.
Revealed only after she had been blindfolded
and made to walk over hitched together interlock in a tight red skirt.
She broke an ankle.

She hated it, him, and the pines on the either side of the entrance
erect as asparagus.
Sedan lobbed in the drive
bratwurst in a neighbourhood
of well-to-do.

She was helpless as a dumb gun.

He poured a Tom Collins
suggested she put her feet up—
he rubbed the very spot that made her sore.
After three Toms she had to confess
she hated the place less, liked the view of the rambling grape vines.
The lone leaf in the pool.

Two dishes left outside when clock rang six
wicked mother-law gift.

And just like that the spell was broken
and he turned into a warty toad
bumpy as the drive over from the apartment where they used to live.

Undone

Naked behind the pool hut
Mama.

He is in love
with the scuttle of the scullions' drowsy walk
wants to liquor-kiss her, everywhere.

On drunken hands and knees he searches for her scent.

Behind the pool hut
two French aprons

and a worn-down path that only the butler knows about.

Thirst for a fling

As finger to crystal rim hums
their bones shook.

Sweet-spots
up their expensive sleeves.

Breathe in
breathe out.

Bored of this house
this sick curious house who drinks too much shade.

Neighbour's loudmouth sunlit faucet
drips, happy.

County cult

Saturday night olive and martini mixer.
Pink paper sky
key bowl
a tussle of shoes.

Sunken living room.
Plush corduroy sectional, half-pie lampshade, frowsy
tangerine shag   and a gold
Peter Jackson cigarette lighter lost in the weeds of its
luxurious hair.

The Hollywood Argyles swing on the electric wheel. Psychedelic
jumble, a tab of pharmacopeia to wind up the shy.
Inside house at the end of the block
a collision of neighbours.

Hymns

To incongruent measures

First

...train track
...two-wheeler
...pair of blue jeans
...well orchestrated lie.

Overdose in her basement—
a pill for that
and the hard manic-depressive days ahead.

A shilling for a pull on the hanging man's legs
before the fallen mask.

The patient is dead.
Therapist talk-talk-talked her fool head right off the collarbone of Friday—

To sugar

He bit off my leg so that I could not run away.
I dragged it to my room.
Crawled under the sheets
stayed there
most of July.

Boarded-up jewel box—
ballerina kink, no twirl.
Hyperkinetic stage fright.

He went to get groceries, bought all I hated—
prunes, lima beans, raw sugar.
Each had a different swallow.

Years later, when my leg grew back
he ignored
the menu of my charm.

I broke his legs.
He crept away on crooked feet and useless hands.

He too
went out rotten—

incurable alcoholic
like my father.

The sorrow of snow

The year I turned 21, I married a corpse.

Drinks first, then
we ate our histories.

Swish swish
Bang bang

We spun-tight lovers on a widow's watch above the drunken orchestra
the waltz of the stark.

Happy fondlers
incomplete.

Cocktail sobriety
clash—

we share a postal address
nothing to say.

House

He owns this living room
its braided carpet, velveteen settee, cone-shaped lampshade
filter cigarettes
and a clock.

I peel and lift a fly's wing off a low table
rid the stain of last night's dark plague
the smell of its whiskey whistle buzz.

Oval coffee table is innocent.

A thousand pesky coils from the ceiling dangle
hands that quick-slap speak.

No bread.
No idea.
Love is a tricky monster with a two-second temper.

The husband

Criminal intent, thrown away embryos—
who made you?

You as in me, us, them, they—
the happy idiot nervosas.

Conception's frisk
stocking feet camouflage
an intruder's slither and slip   hardwood
wet sponge pillow
us.

I am my opiate.
I talk to three-day-old purple balloons.

Husband—
who made you?

To hooks

How unlucky you got through.
The other sperm inside me sank dead.

Husband washed and towelled on a bed of wet-sex-wood
all smiles
and making nice.

In the bathtub I tried to fish you out.

Around the world twice
in the minute it took him to name all the parts of me.

Unscramble all my numb faces.

Of companions

Suspicions grew during those crunchy winter months
that kept communication starved.

Ecstasy's endnote.

Twice hit on the head with hammer.
I got it, slowly.

Each thud made a dent.

Home alone.
A little stronger now, me
a little quieter, not such a braggart.
Two carat diamond—
a finger scab removed.

Three awful days without god

The asphalt aquarium of my innocence wobbled
and became unhinged.

Crouched in the garage
I read the label on a box of toddler-carbs—
folic acid, zinc oxide, vodka, niacin, riboflavin, carbon monoxide.

My mouth tastes like the morning after, plan B.
My hair is an auburn mess
twisting and turning inside my smallclothes.

They caught me running uphill on a one-way street
naked in a new pair of shoes
attempting to outrun mundane.

What time is it,   wolf?

~June~

Calf-slip

stockings, French seam gathered at the nape of her neck

a strand of pearls, cut

span reaching—

liver pâté

Blatherskite across the room wore an acrylic leisure suit with suede elbows—

three-fingers of scotch held by the rim, arms dangled

next to platter

of smoked oysters

Brisk walk through vodka lamplight

she followed

wickedly red entering the Swelter Motel on the edge of town—

out of sorts

just past

switchblade alley

A nibble

of low-cut knowledge—

his half-drowned bird

glinted in the pre-dawn light

the wonder of happenstance

A box of sweet given

she forgot where she lived that entire month of June

~July~

He spoke of God, although, he claimed to be a non-believer

dry clean bones—

where the last of him should have been

old kiss drool

She returned to Clatter hall

~August~

Haystack

at the county fair boring

she-six at the shooting gallery

bobble-heads and heart-shaped candy dishes

won

broken

Prayers for drunks

The day before…

I am a street artist.
Quick hands

sticky sparkles on the city's walled skin.

Monday

I pet the cat.
It bites me.

Sour milk.
I twist its tail.

It bites me again—
this time for good reason.

It can't stop pacing.
I slip into something comfortable—

old slippers, black eyeliner, a claw foot tub.
Wait for sleep.

Tuesday

Bad basement days
gone mouldy

in a container that stinks of me.
I eat mauve popsicles for breakfast.

Wednesday

Voice is a faceless black widow.
Four dead in Plenty.

Mixed up body parts like a shuffled utensil drawer—a row
of dented cans in a supermarket.

Thursday

Jane Doe Syndrome.
Slippery shoes.

Guilt arrives at six.

Presentable
passed hours ago.

Friday

I hail a cab
fumble with my keys in the backseat.

Hand the driver a series of numbered page corners—
Gretel's thorny heels
Cinderella's last dance.

Take me to page 16, I say—
where the *she-six* live.

Saturday

October never happened.

Sunday

Good morning
good intentioned crash-kit in the glove box

out of reach.

Red-eyed passenger.

First Step

I will not drink.
I will not drink today.

I will not drink for today.

The day after. . .

I am
vespula
trapped in cardboard

b
o
x

flares, orange cones—
wreckage.

I will not drink in the morning.

Old Testament

Salt mountain

This communion of home erects itself
alongside stickleback water.

Where the big river sips into
the Lake of Three Spines.

She never liked the taste of Sunday—
its bite-size saviour.

His only daughter
beneath this altar

undressed.

Palms up akin to the curl of a wave.

Prayer beads

nine
shelves of rescue
thirteen Marys

fourteen different
mother tongues
to sink or swim me

rat snake under the fence
bites the neighbour

forgiveness is
a toxic conundrum

six
Guadeloupes
fourteen tongues

to sink
or rescue

snake bite
a form of relief

three
snakes in the garden
six toxic
neighbours

and nine
unforgiving
Mary Magdalenes

Obit for good cupcakes

The moon is in the throat of the wolf pup.
Cupcakes fall from the sky.

A familiar ache
she can't remember.

A lisp-bone predator with a cold orb
is a knot inside house.

Open window—
panic stricken thicket of dirty blonde whores below.

Small host

Close-up his genitals between the folds of the book she never finished. Page numbers were a tight right to text fit. He and she, an open doorway love-thing. Gurgling mouth—he wasn't a cousin exactly—Aunt Dot's relics from the past: a chaste husband, their cranberry Cadillac, three-buttercup Sunday hats. She should have apologized but didn't, instead she offered a wink and kicked the door shut. Lost hatpin between them—

Remedy as cure

A picture he'd taken of her as a tot
daddy's little girl
beautiful baby lips
lower gaze
under the bed

shoebox morphine.

He wasn't allowed in her bedroom after dark.
Mother kept a watch on the children's books that lined the shelves as if they were storm weather.

Everything looks so large when you're small.

Thumbprint as amour-propre.
She put the photo away and returned to the bed where his feet dangled six inches off the floor like two grapefruits.
She mussed his hair, and continued to feed him

shoebox morphine.

Sad Lunatics

Ramble

I am the driver behind the wheel.

Keep going, she says, *out-manoeuvre this array of façades—
clown face storefronts with down-up circular penny staircases
from Plenty's fallen pocket.*

Snapshots of dead relatives scotch-taped to the hooch-man's window.

3, 9, 7
suddenly, the world rights itself.

Green lights twitch everywhere.

Patience's cottage

We ingest cotton gin and jonnycake while we stab waterproof valentines.
Shattered hides in a room
with diamond doorknobs
on a windowsill
where no window was.

We are naughty little houseguests who perch on
dollhouse furniture.
When did we get too big for this life, Patience asks?
It sounds like she's shouting.
Roof shakes.

We rearrange our plaid wingbacks in the screened-in porch so that the neighbours can only see
the backs of our heads.
We tell each other sad stories to cheer ourselves up.
Invention is a full-time job, sorrow much more permanent.

The accident, Patience says…
the baby's fall.

I am so fucking sorry.
I am so fucking sorry.
I am so fucking sorry.
I am so fucking sorry.
I am so fucking sorry.

Idiots shouldn't have babies, I say.
Patience agrees.
She lights a fag, tosses matchstick—
grey smog on the neighbour's lawn.

We are not the forgiving type(s).

Neighbours

At night the neighbour's cottage grows fangs.
Strange sunset when dark kiss comes.

Strap hinge latch.

We can see them whisper.
The rattle of a sharpening wheel
sets in motion
a new kind of boredom.

They spy us.
A scarecrow's sundial companion
tick tocks its shadowy words
as squirrel conspires with crabby windmill.

Chop Chop   off go their heads.

Who locked the neighbours in?

Where are the children?

All the doors are open in the cottage.

A string attached to a foot rocks a chair.
We pretend small visitors.

Up there, Patience says, *they're playing hopscotch in the tree house.*
Watch them fly-skip to the ground, peeled away from the walls.

Such devilish little paint chips.

The pink-shock of their dirty fingers—
now cold in my palm.

Morning

Patience's toenails are blue. Mine are black.
We've
done hard time.
I am fair.
Patience's hair is burnt toast.
We both can't remember how many children we had between us
or where the food is we brought.

Volcanic anthill in the backyard.
Scuttle, drop, scurry.
They never take a day off, their labour
makes us feel guilty.

Neighbour owns a telescopic sky rocket.
He points it.
Patience wears dark sunglasses, eyes glitter purple.
I put on my sunglasses too.
Now they can't see my secrets either.

I ask her if she'd like a pork sandwich.
Yes please, she says.
Good then, so would I.
Neither of us moves.
I can't eat with someone staring at me anyhow.
I nosh a cigarette.

Both of our Mothers are dead now, Fathers too—
we can't remember their surnames.
In the short time we have been sitting, the grass has grown tall.
Queer eyes peer at us—
orange wolf, red badger.

Pounce.

No children

So dark I can't find my gin slipper.
I eat olives, the heads of my enemies.

The feeling to retch returns.
Sick by day.
Better by night.
Patience is asleep
or is she just pretending?
I don't know.
I'm not talking.

I'm barely breathing.

Visitor

Broken string. The chair continues to rock.
Where did that eavesdropping Monster dressed in a smoking jacket who does not like fire-chatter come from?

If the world went quiet
I'd still have—

No gin.
No exit.

The Dead Reinvented

i.

Sweet potato face
a two-penny funerary keepsake on a mantel
a smaller version of what is buried out back.

Windswept shiver.

Is that you?
Is that me who looks at you the same, but different?

Time shudder.

I came to you with a bag of marble stone and a secret in my pocket.

ii.

Is it really that easy to bury the young?

Pray   work   pray.
Repeat the words for   cholera   skin-peel.

Two forks, two knives, and three little spoons traipse through
a corridor at the bottom of a staircase where the sleepwalkers carry
rust in their lunchboxes.

Their hands so small they make their parents cry. Make them want to take back the
wishes they wasted on themselves.

iii.

Are we not the keepers of small songs?

iv.

Chicken has a glass eye
and a look of flash hook fright.
Three dead crows, a goat, and a plough horse buried
in a well. Desperate times
religion's thirst has a new worm in the belly.

v.

O little box of soap
on the sill where mama used to bathe him.
All dried up
mama's helper, apple peeler, messenger-boy gone wild
ran off toward the great big sky.

vi.

Papa set the house on fire to drive away the plague.
To err is a matchstick, a book of good learning
and mama's burnt shoes—
before the stairs collapsed.

vii.

The boy took sick three days after he had mastered the alphabet.
Not enough house to wash his shirt proper.
Stuffed in someone else's coat
boy slumped in a hundred-year-old chair, mouth tipped slightly open, hand on the armrest as though poised to answer a question.
Painted-on eyes and cheeks
buttons larger than his entire life.

viii.

Pretty girls return to the soil in satin gloves
on a song of leaves.

They carry their gentle ringlets.

O Sacred Skeletal Mountain of cream clotted lullabies—

                your body
                                your lovely.

Little boys down from the hills to worship their petrified gowns.

ix.

A cup of birth in a grainy glass frame
a thin shy hand reaches upward from the riverbed to rock
your chubby white bones home.

x.

Limp arm draped over a dead brother's left shoulder.
Rose settee, Asian flowerpot.
Twin chimney sweeps dressed in matching suits so snug they look born into them.

A month's pay is a half-cup of cold lung soup.

Go Home Lake

Taken

Holy commuter
well-situated.
his turn around lie

Jackstay, road split
his seduction's thirst.
bundle-board

West to water
deflowered.
the Book of Ruth

Fish on a highway, net, sea
hooked into.
virgin catch of the day

Expectation answered—
the Southern Line don't wave.
question dismissed

Long skirts, chary they peddle
from the carnivore of Sunday.
turn away

Jack-in-the-pulpit
impala lyre.
bog onion, brown dragon, Indian turnip

Funnel cloud
tree swallow.
savvy whip

Storm to name her
alone to Go Home Lake.
braid and cap, slip-clutch

The distance between every boozy sadness is her beauty

Death came to collect her.
The door was locked.

She refused to accept the murky bliss
of spontaneous domesticity.

Patience took back her hours
slept dirty when she wanted
kept wild in the nightstand.

A white cockroach in the aquarium
men in the throat
women under the bed.

Blue crypt

They were born with little feet
slow to crawl
the Bathwater Babies.

For them
dying was temporary
an amethyst flame.

Payback for a whore's bite and wasp's sting.

Bratstone tongue pried from plush.
This is where the truth lives.

Bone and dust muzzled into concrete
they arrive naked and on their backs.

They refuse to share their ashes with our earth.

Who shan't escape

A pale witness picks up a cigarette and lights its final inhale.
Quitters live in a wasteland.

Sway and stoop.

Cemetery gate is open, nothing gets in.
Not even the twice dead.
The man who choked on a rat snake
the man who messed with Eden.

Like a shotgun awaits a prayer
it will take years for the city to mend.

At the end of dirt

In a spirit of your own personality
happiness is a birth defect.

The badge of random authority—
yes-men
blue market slaves
the twine of body physics
bloodletting
and
soft cranium drills.

The hunger of feet—the hunger
of dogs.
Starvation's
hypnotic fugue.

Prepare the noose.
Knot the sheets.

Harpist's quarters

Hollow rush
oxygen whimsy.
The dead are among us—
their handprints faint but recognizable through the soot of old French panes in a certain angle of light.

Look up.
Here
a bridge of a thousand fingers
at the crossing.

Sinister click
séance deadbolt
and a candelabra possess perpendicular thought.

Dial back
to the rooms of ugly
garnished with luxurious fabrics imported from The Northern Line.

House servants: six for a penny.
In an ivory kitchen is a choir in chains.

Out back in a laboratory cage—

slice and contort
facial-horror
human-scab.

Bones buried in the courtyard walls.
Patience's wide dress sweeps the overflow from stemless flute glasses—

silver caviar
prim linen.

Caesarean keeper: mother kills twelve-year-old before she bleeds.

Oleanders skitter to the sidewalk.
A gilt carriage trots.

Who knows for sure who haunts this place?

Acknowledgements

The collection was initially inspired by the works of Anne Sexton. "Three awful days without god" originally called "Vacant Hymn" was inspired by Sexton's mental breakdown and subsequent hospitalization. The poem first appeared in the anthology *A Crystal Through Which Love Passes, Glosas for P.K. Page*, Buschek Books, 2012.

"Blue" first appeared in *BafterC*, Book Thug, 2014. The fabled town of Blue is modelled after Westport, Ontario, (the village of seven churches) my maternal side's ancestral home. "Clatter Hall" was inspired by the LDS community, (Latter Day Saints).

The section "Go Home Lake" is dedicated to the Black slaves of the Delphine LaLaurie household, the French Quarter, circa 1834.

The poem "Taken" was written for the two little Amish girls who were abducted from a roadside flower stand in Upper New York State, summer 2014. They were safety found.

"The Dead Reinvented" was inspired by *Momento Mori*, by Dan Meinwald, and his collection of nineteenth century funerary photographs depicting the dearly departed.

The poem "County Cult" originally titled, "Flag of Another Country", first appeared on the Chaudiere Books blog for National Poetry Month 2015. From the street I watched as people danced naked, Kingston, Ontario, circa 1973.

"Sad Lunatics" is based on an imaginary psychedelic road trip between the poet Sexton and Patience. As well as my aunts, Cat and Ann, who taught me to be stealth, resourceful, believe in the supernatural and the power within.

A heartfelt thanks to the extraordinary women I met at E Fry. Your stories of surviving incest inspired me. The section "Old Testament" is dedicated to you brave women!

Thank you to The Toronto New School of Writing, and Phil Hall in particular for guiding me through the psychological labyrinth of this collection.

Much gratitude to the Ontario Arts Council.

Mind-blowing thanks to the Kingston Writing community for their support—especially Laurie Lewis and Jeanette Lynes.

High-five to Sandra Ridley for improving the editing score of these poems and Christine McNair for the funky cover and awesome layout. Thanks to rob and Christine at Chaudiere Books for giving this manuscript a soap box from which to perch.

A big whoop for Jake for the author photo!

Jennifer Londry is the author of two books of poetry: *Life and Death in Cheap Motels*, which was adapted for stage, and *After the Words*, which was nominated for a Saskatchewan Book Award. A featured reader at the 2009 Kingston Writers' Festival and at the 2011 Sweetwater 905 in Northern BC, she has also facilitated and organized a literary event for Alzheimer's Awareness. Jen has taught creative writing and recently was a judge for Words from the Street, a creative writing competition, which gives a voice to the downtrodden, in association with The Toronto Writers' Collective. She is also a contributor to the anthologies: *A Crystal through which Love Passes, Glosas for P.K. Page* (Buschek Books, 2013), *Where the nights Are twice As long, Love Letters of Canadian Poets* (Goose Lane Editions, 2015), and has work forthcoming in the Alzheimer's anthology, *A Rewording Life*, editor Diane Schoemperlen, creator Sheryl Gordon. Currently Jen is collaborating with the documentary filmmaker Sarah Turnbull at the Carleton School of Journalism and Communications to produce a mental health video.

Colophon

Typeset in Joanna MT by Christine McNair in Adobe InDesign. Joanna was designed by Eric Gill in 1930, based on type originally cut by Granjon, and released by the Monotype Corporation in 1937. He created the typeface for the printing firm of Hague & Gill, which he formed to give his idle son-in-law an occupation, and named the design for his daughter. It is, as Gill himself described it, "a book face free from all fancy business."

Library and Archives Canada Cataloguing in Publication

Londry, Jennifer, author
Tatterdemalion / Jennifer Londry.

Poems.
ISBN 978-1-928107-05-7 (paperback)

I. Title.

PS8623.O495T38 2015 C811'.6 C2015-906148-2

WWW.CHAUDIEREBOOKS.COM